FAST FACTS

Incredible Human Body

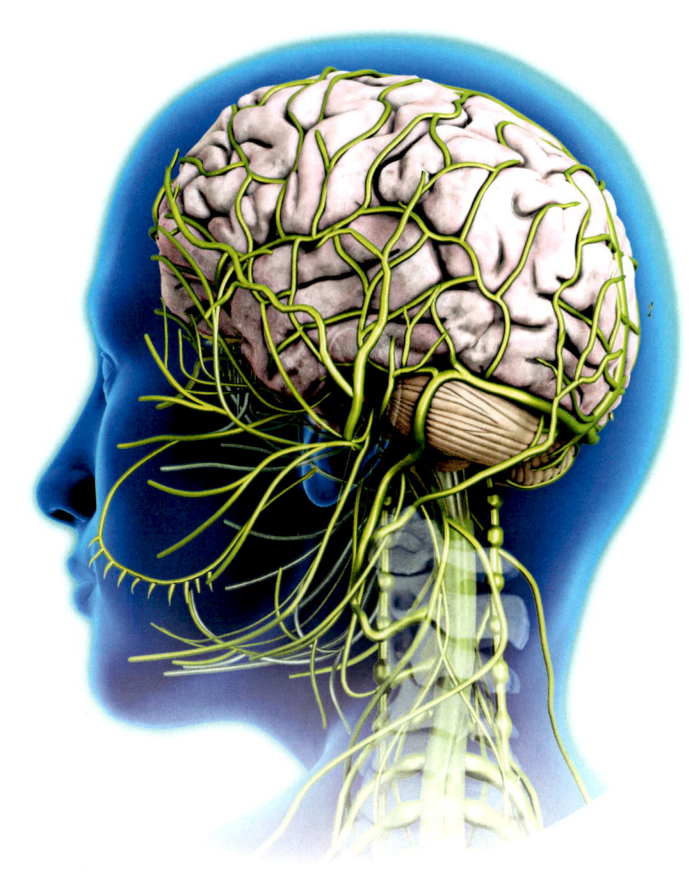

 **KINGFISHER**

First published 2016 by Kingfisher
an imprint of Macmillan Children's Books
20 New Wharf Road, London N1 9RR
Associated companies throughout the world
www.panmacmillan.com

Copyright © Macmillan Publishers International Ltd 2016

Interior design by Tall Tree Ltd
Cover design by Peter Clayman

Adapted from an original text by Miranda Smith
Literacy consultants: Kerenza Ghosh, Stephanie Laird

ISBN 978-0-7534-3976-0

All rights reserved. No part of this publication may be reproduced, stored in or introduced into a retrieval system, or transmitted, in any form or by any means (electronic, mechanical, photocopying, recording or otherwise), without the prior written permission of the publisher. Any person who does any unauthorized act in relation to this publication may be liable to criminal prosecution and civil claims for damages.

A CIP catalogue record for this book is available from the British Library.

Printed in China

9 8 7 6 5 4 3 2 1
1TR/0516/WKT/UG/128MA

This book is sold subject to the condition that it shall not, by way of trade or otherwise, be lent, resold, hired out, or otherwise circulated without the publisher's prior consent in any form of binding or cover other than that in which it is published and without a similar condition including this condition being imposed on the subsequent purchaser.

Picture credits
The Publisher would like to thank the following for permission to reproduce their material.
Top = t; Bottom = b; Centre = c; Left = l; Right = r
Front cover Shutterstock/Sebastian Kaulitzki; background Shutterstock/Sergey Nivens; Back cover iStock/Ferran Traite Soler; Pages 6–7 Corbis/Randy Faris; 7tr SPL/Alfred Pasieka; 9cr SPL/BSIP, Chassenet; 10tr Shutterstock; 10bl SPL/Steve Gschmeissner; 10br Shutterstock; 10–11 Corbis/Kai Pfaffenbach/Reuters; 11ct Shutterstock; 11c Shutterstock; 11bl Shutterstock; 11br Shutterstock; 12cl SPL/Steve Gschmeissner; 12bc Getty/Taxi; 12cr iStock/7activestudio; 13br SPL/Andrew Syred; 14b SPL; 15cl SPL/Steve Gschmeissner; 16br SPL/Susumu Nishinaga; 17tl iStock/william97; 17cl Corbis/Visuals Unlimited; 17bl SPL/John Bavosi; 18tr iStock/ktsimage; 19c Alamy/Zoonar GmbH; 19cl Getty/Visuals Unlimited; 19br SPL/Eye of Science; 23t iStock/martinasphotography; 24tr SPL/Alex Bartel; 25tc SPL/Eye of Science; 25t SPL/Alain Pol, ISM; 26cr SPL/Robert Brocksmith; 27t SPL/Professor P Motta/Dept of Anatomy/La Sapienza, Rome; 28–29 SPL/Pasieka; 29br SPL/Pasieka

Contents

4 The body machine

6 A framework of bones

8 Muscles in action

10 Moving parts

12 Body protection

14 The body motor

16 Take a breath

18 Body messengers

20 The control centre

22 Five senses

24 What happens to your food?

26 Building blocks

28 Special instructions

30 Glossary

32 Index

The body machine

The human body has many parts that all help to keep it working. Your body contains ten internal body systems that act together to make everything run smoothly. On the outside are skin, hair and nails, which make up the system that covers and protects the body.

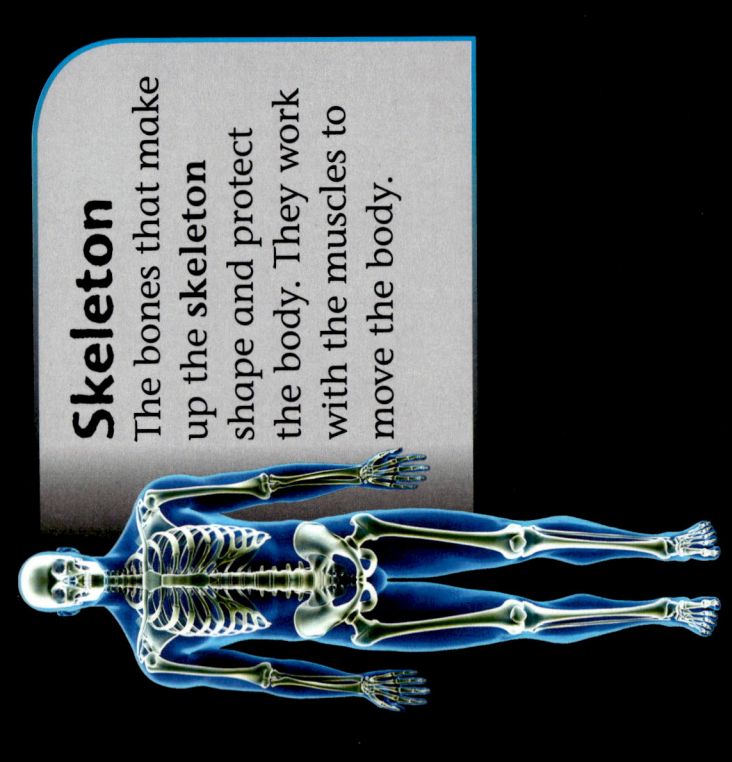

Skeleton
The bones that make up the skeleton shape and protect the body. They work with the muscles to move the body.

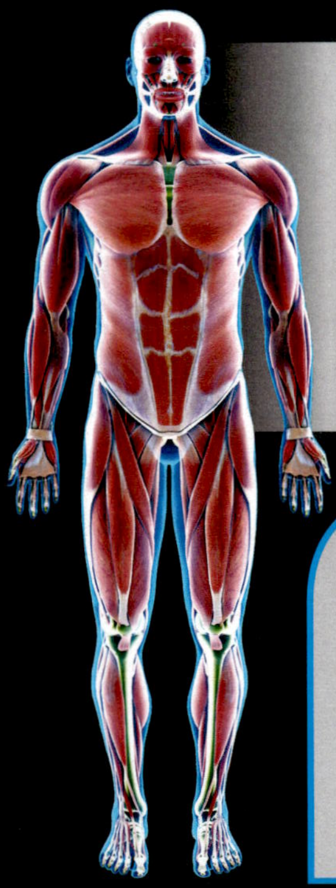

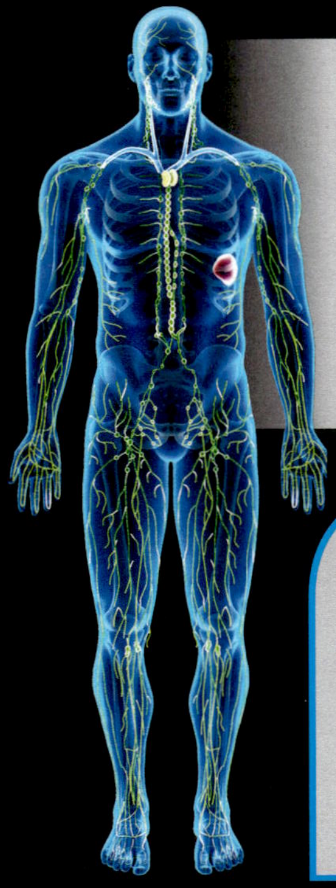

Lymph
The lymph system balances the body's fluids and helps fight infection.

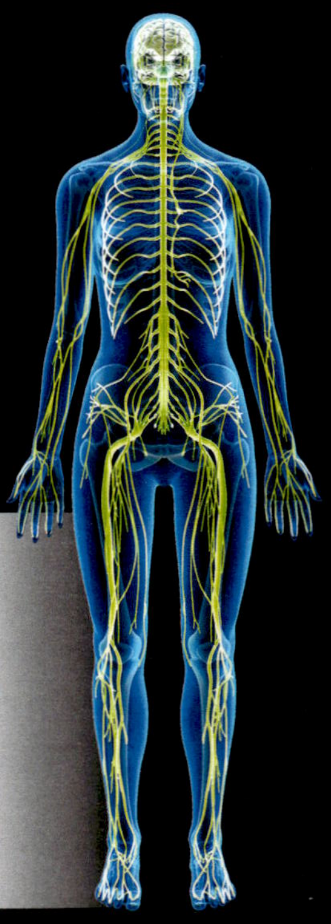

Nerves
The nervous system carries signals to and from the brain and spinal cord.

Muscles
Muscles control the movement of bones and some of the internal organs.

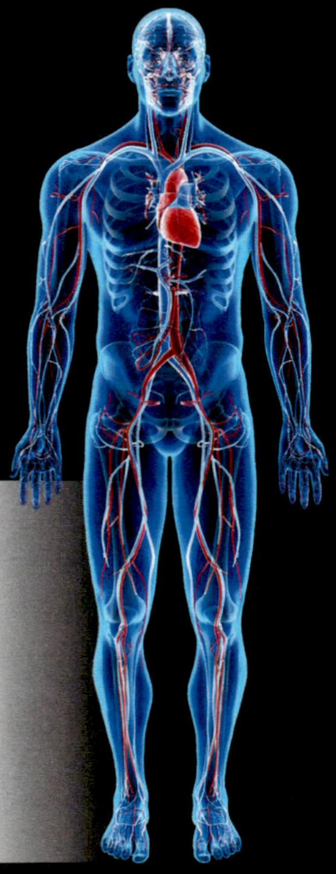

Blood
The cardiovascular system carries blood around the body, pushed by the heart.

Breathing

The lungs take in oxygen from the air into the blood and get rid of unwanted carbon dioxide.

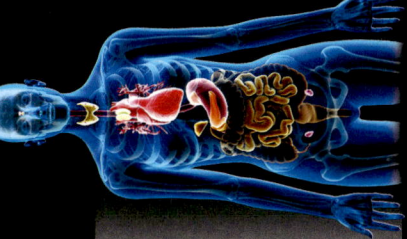

Hormones

Hormones control body processes such as growth. They are produced by organs dotted around the body.

Intestines

This system processes nutrients from the food you eat and gets rid of unwanted food through the anus.

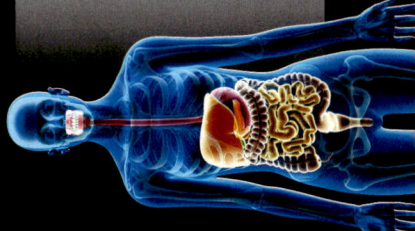

Urine

The kidneys filter waste products out of the blood and make urine, which leaves the body through the bladder.

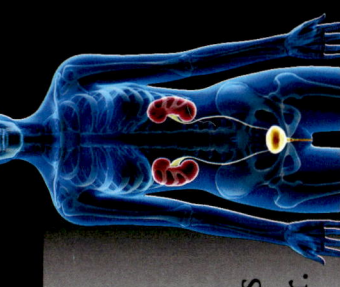

Reproduction

The male reproductive organs produce sperm. The female reproductive organs produce eggs. The female body can also carry and nourish a baby until it is ready to be born.

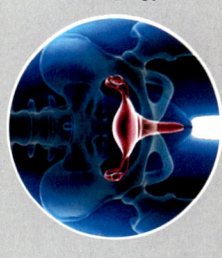 Female reproductive system

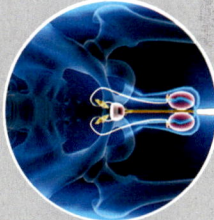 Male reproductive system

system
A group of organs and tissues that perform a particular body function.

TOP FIVE BITESIZE FACTS

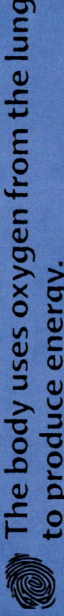 The body uses oxygen from the lungs to produce energy.

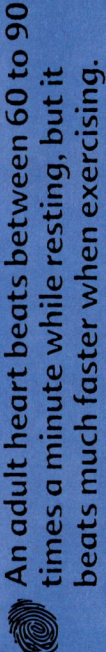 An adult heart beats between 60 to 90 times a minute while resting, but it beats much faster when exercising.

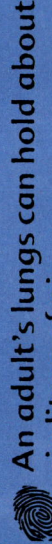 An adult's lungs can hold about six litres of air.

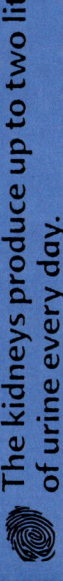 The kidneys produce up to two litres of urine every day.

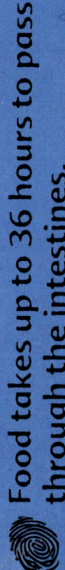 Food takes up to 36 hours to pass through the intestines.

A framework of bones

The skeleton is the rigid framework of bones that supports and shapes the body. The bones vary in size and function. Long bones are found in the limbs and help us to move. Flat bones and irregular bones protect the organs.

The hip bones are fused together to form the pelvis.

Bone structure
At the centre of a long bone is a cavity, or space, filled with **bone marrow**. All bones contain blood vessels, nerve **cells** and living bone cells, which make the bone and store minerals until they are needed.

Skeletal system
Without a skeleton, the human body would not be able to move, and its vital organs would have no protection. The skeleton and muscles work together to move the body.

The fibula is the calf bone at the back of your lower leg.

The tibia is the shin bone at the front of your lower leg.

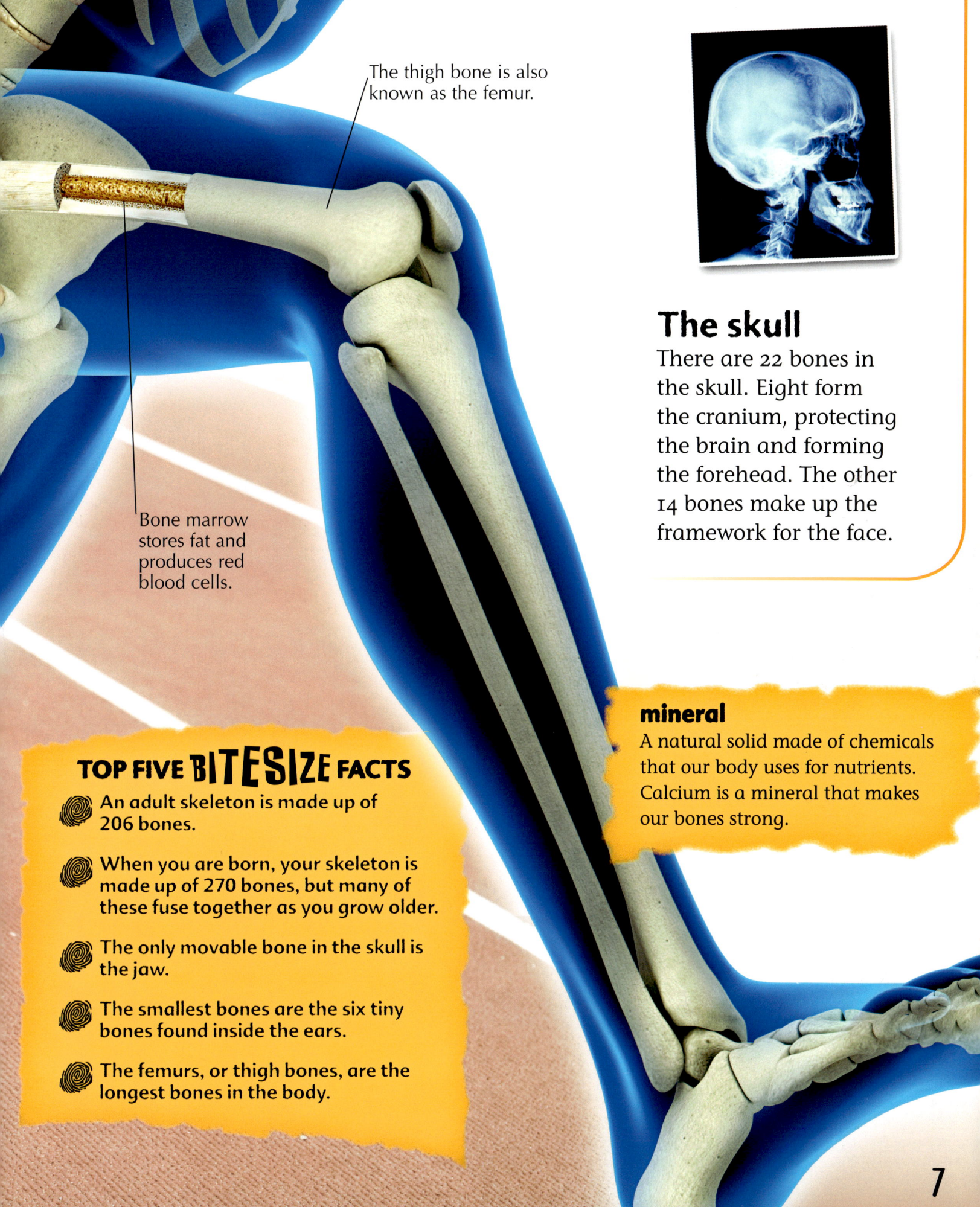

The thigh bone is also known as the femur.

Bone marrow stores fat and produces red blood cells.

The skull
There are 22 bones in the skull. Eight form the cranium, protecting the brain and forming the forehead. The other 14 bones make up the framework for the face.

mineral
A natural solid made of chemicals that our body uses for nutrients. Calcium is a mineral that makes our bones strong.

TOP FIVE BITESIZE FACTS

- An adult skeleton is made up of 206 bones.
- When you are born, your skeleton is made up of 270 bones, but many of these fuse together as you grow older.
- The only movable bone in the skull is the jaw.
- The smallest bones are the six tiny bones found inside the ears.
- The femurs, or thigh bones, are the longest bones in the body.

Muscles in action

Muscles help to keep you upright and stop your joints from coming apart. They keep your heart beating, your stomach working and your body moving. All muscles get shorter to pull a body part into position.

Muscle system
Every movement of the body is created by muscles. There are three kinds of muscle: skeletal, smooth and cardiac. They cover the body in layers, and most of them are skeletal muscles.

Leg work
When you run, the muscles in your legs work together to lift each leg in turn, straightening and bending the knees and changing the position of the feet. All muscles contract and pull; they cannot push. Therefore muscles are arranged in pairs that work in opposition to one another. When one muscle contracts, the other relaxes.

fibre
A part of a plant or animal that is shaped like string.

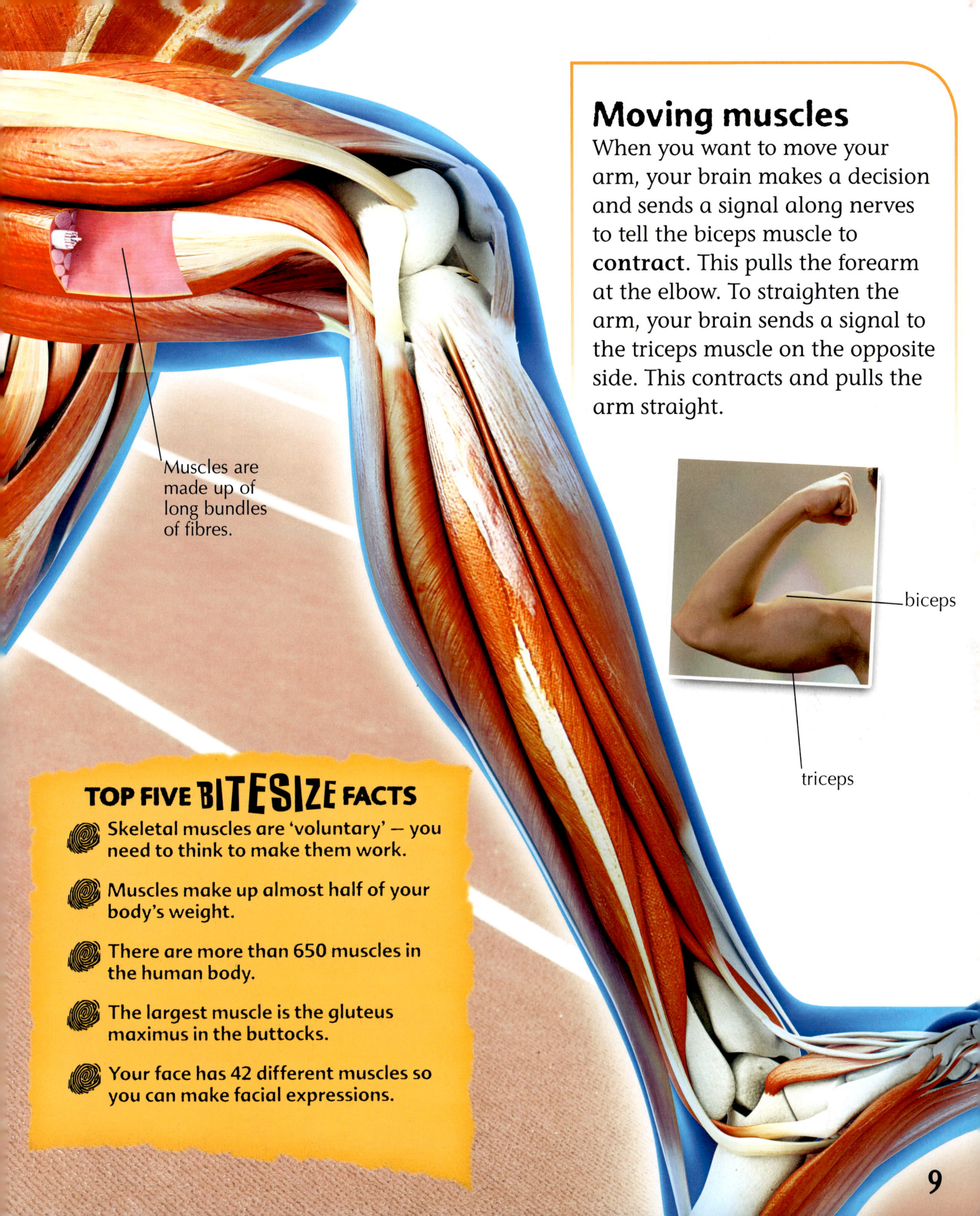

Muscles are made up of long bundles of fibres.

Moving muscles

When you want to move your arm, your brain makes a decision and sends a signal along nerves to tell the biceps muscle to **contract**. This pulls the forearm at the elbow. To straighten the arm, your brain sends a signal to the triceps muscle on the opposite side. This contracts and pulls the arm straight.

biceps

triceps

TOP FIVE BITESIZE FACTS

- Skeletal muscles are 'voluntary' — you need to think to make them work.
- Muscles make up almost half of your body's weight.
- There are more than 650 muscles in the human body.
- The largest muscle is the gluteus maximus in the buttocks.
- Your face has 42 different muscles so you can make facial expressions.

Moving parts

While muscles pull on bones, the bones themselves move around joints. Your body has different types of joint for different movements.

Joints and movement

Most of the body's joints are synovial joints, which are very mobile. There are six types of synovial joint. The largest of all is the knee, which is a hinge joint. The shoulder is a ball-and-socket joint, which allows movement in all directions.

A hinge joint is where one bone fits into a space in another bone, a bit like a puzzle piece.

Ligaments

These are tough, fibrous cords of tissue that hold bones together at a joint. They are not elastic, but they are flexible. They protect and stabilize joints by limiting their movement. This magnified view shows the strong fibres (pink) that make up a ligament.

Plane, or gliding, joints are where both bones are flattened and slide over each other.

In a ball-and-socket joint, the round head of one bone fits into the cup-like end of another.

TOP FIVE BITESIZE FACTS

- A joint is where two bones meet.
- Your spine is made up of 33 different bones called vertebrae. Each vertebra is joined to the next one by a type of plane joint.
- You are about one centimetre shorter at night because your joints compress during the day.
- Some joints, such as those in the skull, don't allow any movement.
- In many joints, the bone ends are covered with **cartilage** to protect them and keep things moving smoothly.

The end of one bone turns within the ring-shaped socket of another to form a pivot joint.

In an ellipsoid joint, the egg-shaped end of one bone fits into a cavity on another.

In a saddle joint, each bone has a curved edge, like a saddle, so the bones can slide back and forth and rotate.

pivot
To pivot is to turn around or move back and forth.

11

Body protection

The human body is covered by skin, which protects you from infection and damage. Hairs help to control body temperature along with sweat **glands** in the skin. Nails cover and protect the sensitive tips of your fingers and toes.

Hair on the head preserves heat, and cushions against impact.

Skin layers

Your skin has three main layers. The outer layer is called the epidermis and is made up of layers of cells that wear away and are renewed. Below this is the dermis, which contains touch sensors and glands that produce oily sebum. The final layer is called subcutaneous tissue and it contains sweat glands and fat cells.

enlarged view of skin cells

Hairs grow from hair bulbs, or roots, deep in the skin. The part of the hair you can see above the skin is called the hair shaft.

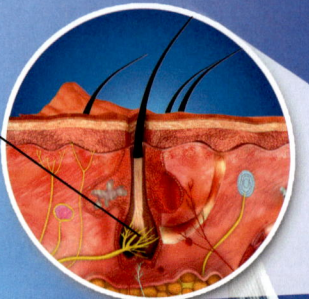

Skin surface

These cells on the skin surface are about to flake off, while new cells move up from the bottom of the epidermis to take their place. This outer layer is made up of dead cells.

Skin colour

The colour of skin depends on how much **melanin** it contains. Melanin coloration is decided by the **DNA** of the person and by how much the skin is exposed to the sun.

touch sensors
Sensors in the skin that send nerve signals to the brain.

touch sensors in the dermis (blue) epidermis (red)

TOP FIVE BITESIZE FACTS

- Skin is the largest organ in your body.
- Hair shafts are made from dead cells and a hard protein called **keratin**.
- Cells in the epidermis are completely replaced every 28 days.
- The sebum produced by the skin helps to stop the hairs and skin drying out.
- Sweat glands under the skin produce **perspiration** to cool you down.

fingernail
cuticle
nail root
bone
fat

Nail growth
As the nails grow, the cells below the nail root move up towards the surface, pressing tightly together. The cells pile up in layers of keratin, which make up the nail.

The body motor

valve
A lid-like structure that opens and closes to control the flow of a liquid.

Blood flows through the body in tubes called **blood vessels**. **Arteries** lead to arterioles, which narrow into **capillaries**. These then lead into **veins** that return blood to the heart.

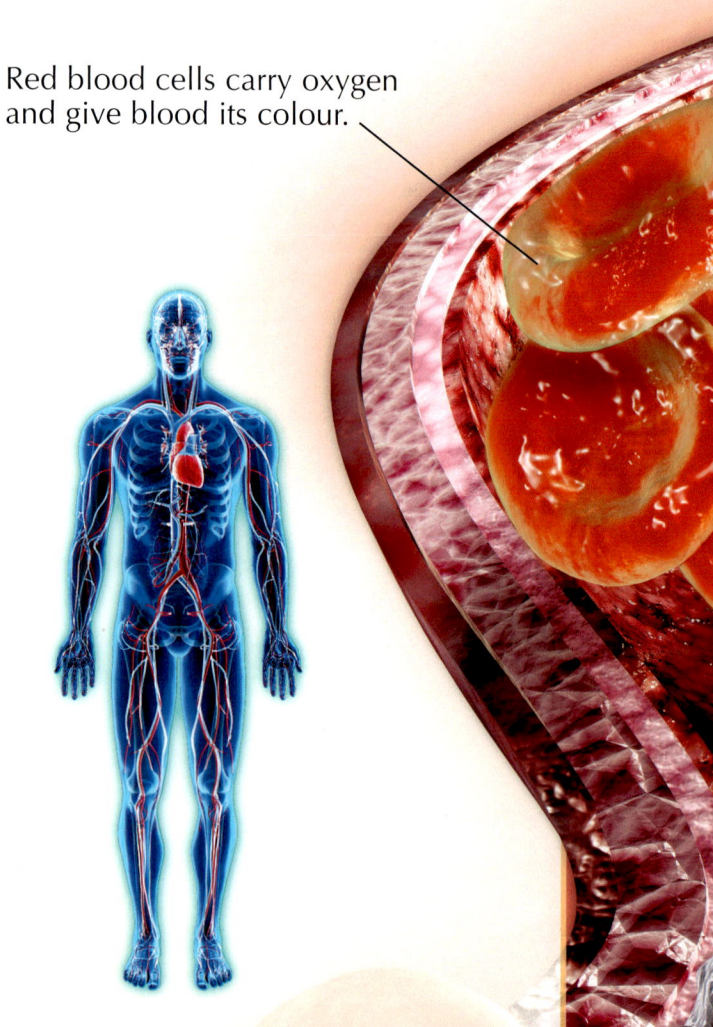

Red blood cells carry oxygen and give blood its colour.

How the heart works

The heart is made up of a special kind of muscle – cardiac muscle. This pumps the blood through four hollow chambers, which each have one-way valves between them that keep the blood flowing in the right direction. The upper chambers are called atria and the lower chambers are called ventricles.

atria
ventricles

Cardiovascular system

This system consists of the heart, blood vessels and the blood itself. It transports the blood, carrying it away from the heart through arteries, and carrying blood back to the heart through veins.

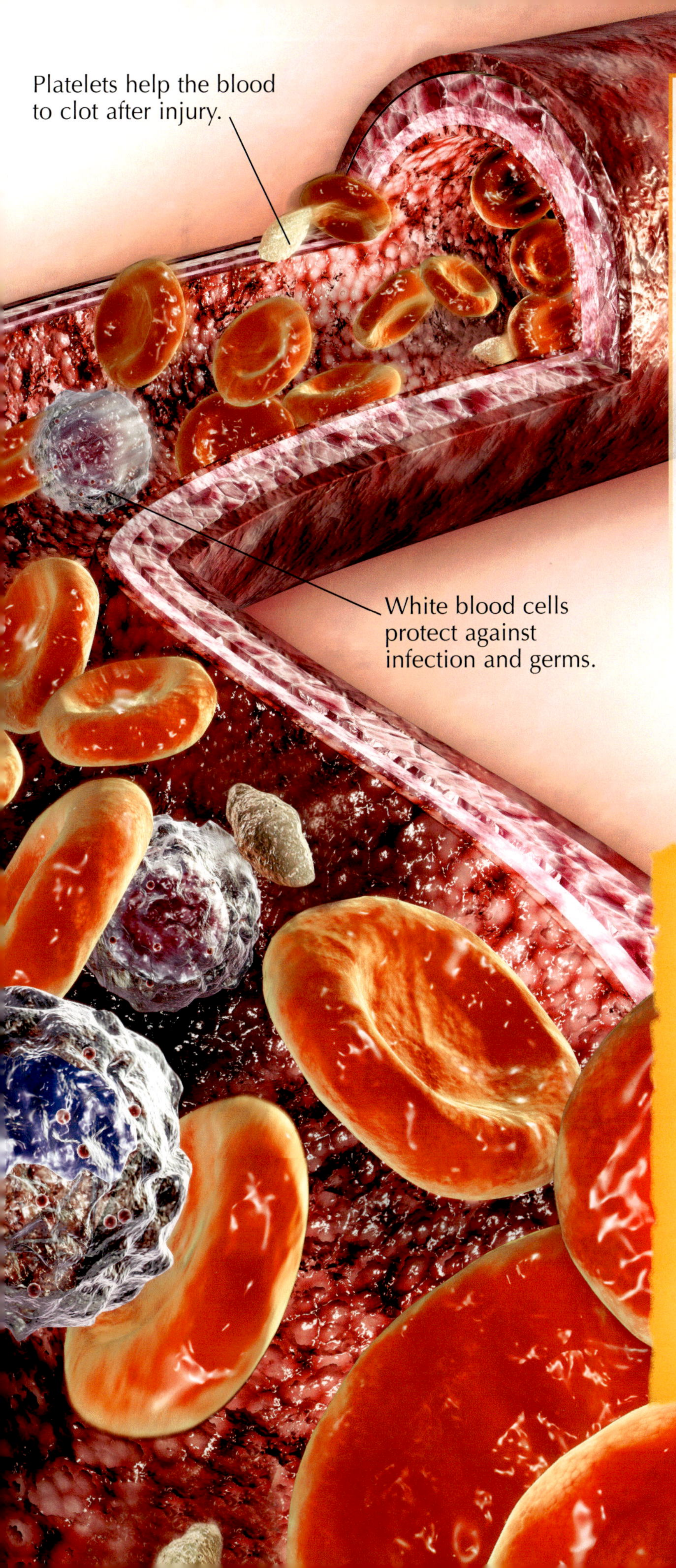

Platelets help the blood to clot after injury.

White blood cells protect against infection and germs.

Blood clotting

Platelets help bleeding to stop. They become sticky and clump together to seal off the wound. They also release chemicals that trap blood cells and other platelets to form a clot. The clot dries on the skin's surface to become a scab.

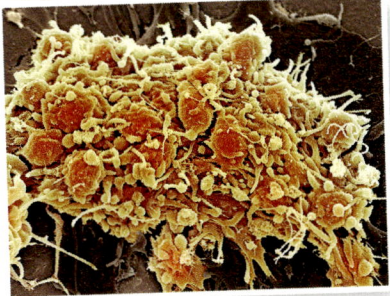

magnified view of a clump of platelets

TOP FIVE BITESIZE FACTS

- Adult humans have five to six litres of blood flowing through their blood vessels.

- A person's heart is about the same size as a clenched fist.

- Plasma is the fluid that makes up about 50 per cent of blood.

- Your body makes about 100 billion red blood cells every hour.

- Laid out end to end, the blood vessels in an average adult human would stretch about 160,000 kilometres — about four times around the world!

Take a breath

Your body needs oxygen and you get this from the air you breathe. Your body also needs to get rid of carbon dioxide. This exchange of gases takes place inside your lungs, which sit inside your chest.

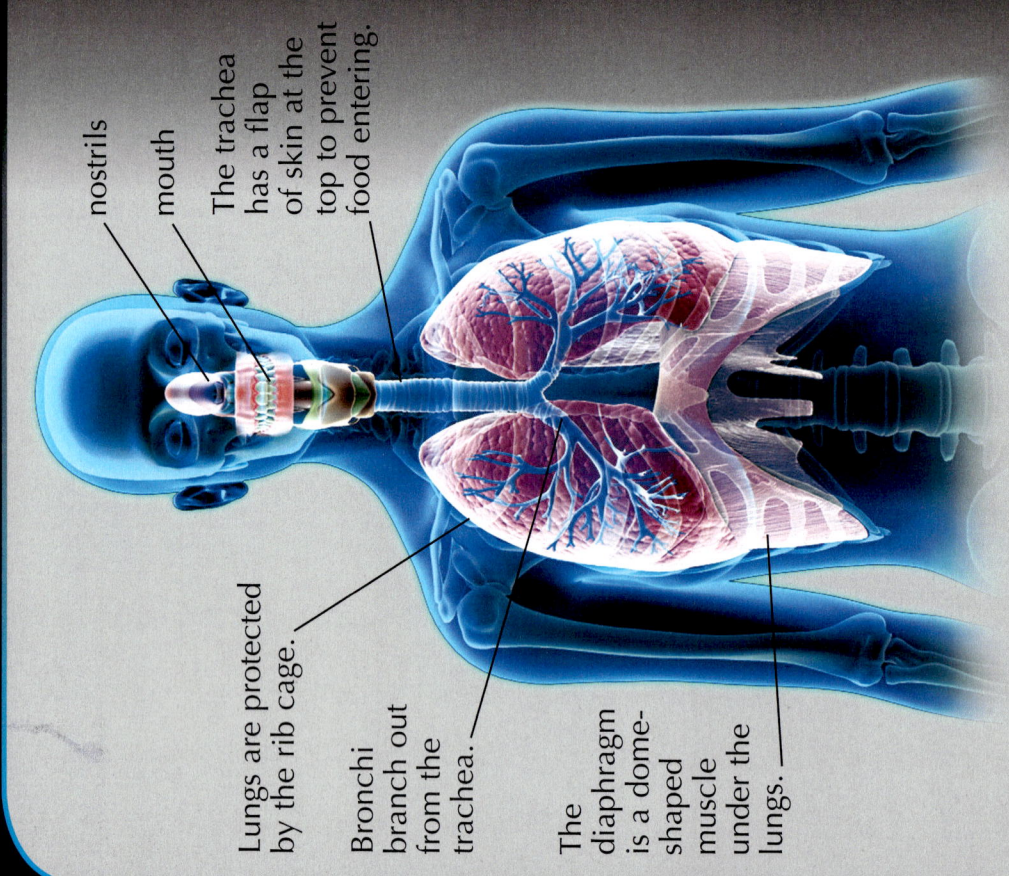

nostrils

mouth

The trachea has a flap of skin at the top to prevent food entering.

Lungs are protected by the rib cage.

Bronchi branch out from the trachea.

The diaphragm is a dome-shaped muscle under the lungs.

How it works
Your nose, throat, larynx (voice box), trachea and lungs all make up the respiratory system. When you inhale (breathe in), you draw in air through your nostrils and mouth and fill the lungs with oxygen-rich air. This oxygen, which is vital to the body, is transferred to the blood.

The trachea
The trachea, or windpipe, is a tube made out of rings of cartilage that help to keep your airways open. The trachea contains **mucus**-secreting glands, such as the one shown here. The glands add moisture to the air as it passes through.

airways
The passages inside a human or animal body through which air travels.

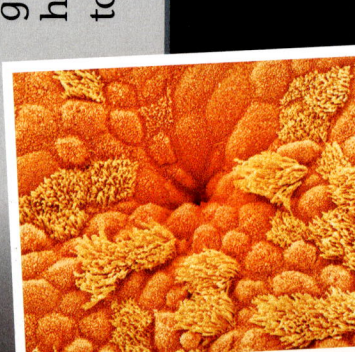

Inhaling and exhaling

When you inhale, the diaphragm moves down and the muscles between your ribs pull outwards. This sucks air in and inflates your lungs. When you exhale (breathe out), the diaphragm and the muscles relax to push the air back out.

Exercise makes you breathe harder and faster to get more oxygen into your body.

TOP FIVE BITESIZE FACTS

- Each lung contains up to 400 million tiny alveoli.
- If laid out, the area made up by all your alveoli would cover a tennis court.
- The network of bronchi, bronchioles and alveoli is called the bronchial tree.
- Your right lung is shorter than your left because it has to make room for the liver.
- Your left lung is slimmer than your right to make room for your heart.

lifelike model of the lungs

An alveolus is lined with a single layer of cells.

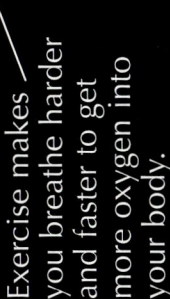

The sac shape of an alveolus provides a large surface area to allow gases to pass through more easily.

Branches

In the lungs, the bronchi divide into smaller tubes called bronchioles. These end in tiny sacs called alveoli. The alveoli are just one cell thick and are surrounded by tiny capillaries. Oxygen from inside the lungs can pass easily through this thin barrier and into the blood, while carbon dioxide passes from the blood and into the lungs.

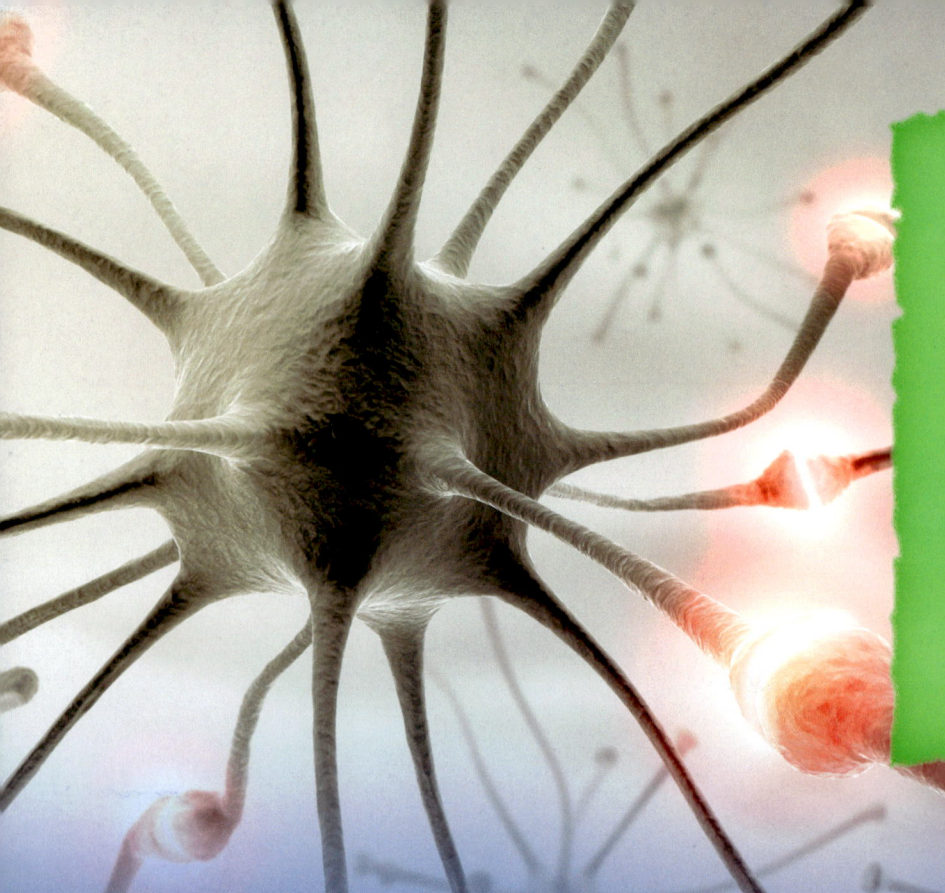

TOP FIVE BITESIZE FACTS

- Some axons can be one metre long.
- Some parts of your body have more nerve endings than others. Your fingertips have lots, so they are very sensitive.
- Nerve signals travel through the body at about 400 kilometres per hour.
- An axon can carry 2500 nerve signals every second.
- The chemicals released across a synapse are called neurotransmitters.

Body messengers

Nerve cells, or **neurons**, carry messages all over the body. There are three types: sensory neurons, interneurons and motor neurons. Sensory neurons are stimulated by touch, taste, smell, sound and sight. Interneurons pass messages on to other nerve cells. Motor neurons send signals to muscles and glands, telling them to carry out actions.

Nervous system

This vast network of neurons transmits messages all over the human body via nerve signals. The brain and the spinal cord form the central nervous system. This works without stopping, collecting information and sending out messages that result in bodily activity.

Neurons

Each neuron has a cell body with short 'feelers' called dendrites. These pick up nerve signals from nearby neurons. A long nerve fibre, the axon, then carries the impulses away to be picked up by the dendrites of other neurons. This picture shows a magnified cut-through view of neurons.

Nerve impulses

When stimulated, neurons produce waves of electricity – nerve impulses. These impulses travel down the axon of the nerve to its junction with another nerve or cell.

At synapses, the nerve impulses are converted into a chemical message.

impulse
An electrical signal that carries messages between the brain and the body.

The chemicals are released and cross the gap at a synapse to pass the message on.

Synapses

Here, two branching nerve fibres (purple) can be seen connecting to the surface of a neuron. The junctions where they meet are called **synapses**. Impulses run down the fibres into the neuron, and this stimulates the cell. Impulses cross from one neuron to another at synapses.

The control centre

Your brain is the centre of the nervous system that controls everything, from thinking to blinking. The bundle of nerve fibres that makes up the spinal cord reaches from the brain right down the length of your back. It carries messages between the brain and the nerves in the rest of the body.

How the brain works

When you read, the information is passed from the eyes to the largest part of the brain, the cerebrum. This part is used for thinking, reasoning and memorizing. It also controls muscle movements. If you read a funny book, the brain transmits that information via the nervous system, and you exercise those muscles that make you laugh.

Grey and white matter

The tissue of the cerebrum has two layers. The outer, grey layer is the cerebral cortex, known as grey matter. The inner layer, or white matter, is made up mainly of nerve fibres.

grey matter

white matter

cerebrum

The cerebellum ('little brain') controls balance, limb movement and coordination.

The brain stem connects the brain to the spinal column.

20

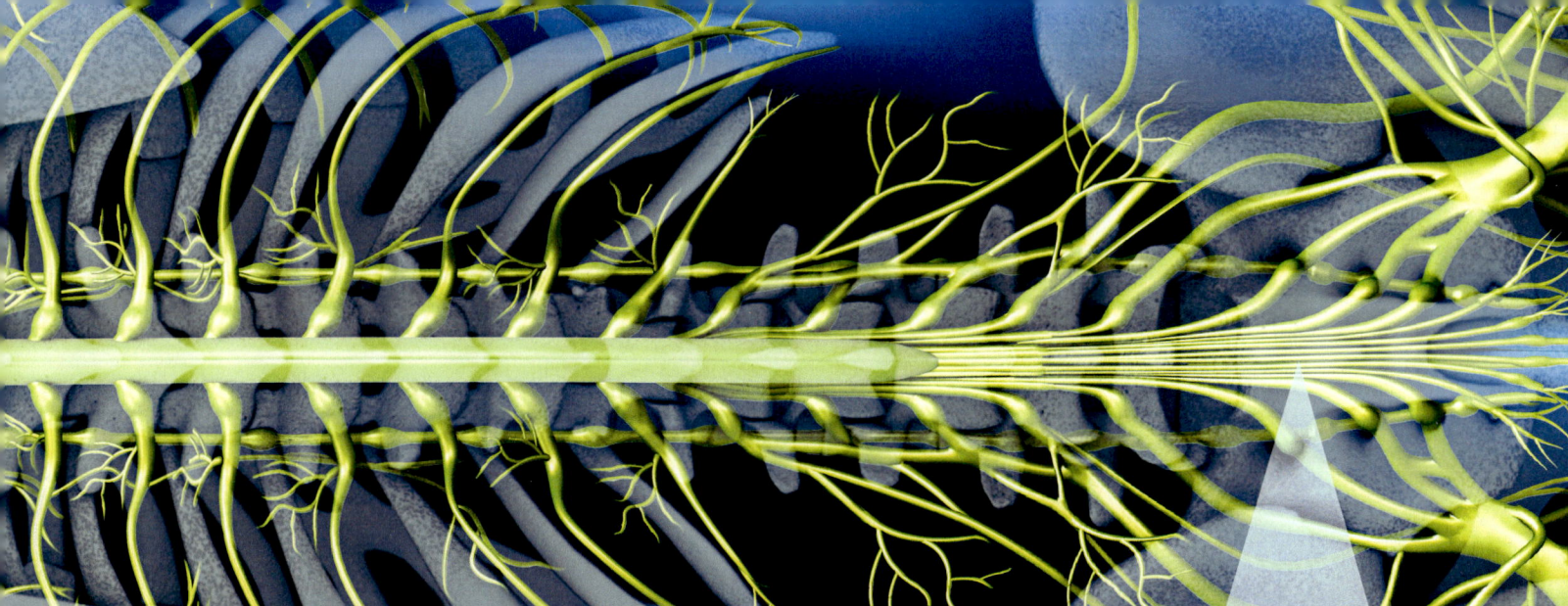

TOP FIVE BITESIZE FACTS

- The brain is protected by three membranes, known as the meninges, as well as the hard skull.
- The left half of the cerebrum controls the right side of the body, and the right half controls the left side.
- An adult brain weighs 1.4 kilograms.
- The brain makes up 2 per cent of body weight, but it uses 20 per cent of the body's energy.
- A human brain contains about 100 billion nerve cells.

The spinal cord

The cord is protected by a flexible spinal column made up of bones called vertebrae. A clear fluid surrounds the cord and acts as a cushion, protecting the nerve tissues against damage.

vertebra

spinal nerve

grey matter

white matter

grey matter
The surface layer of the cerebrum and the inner part of the spinal cord.

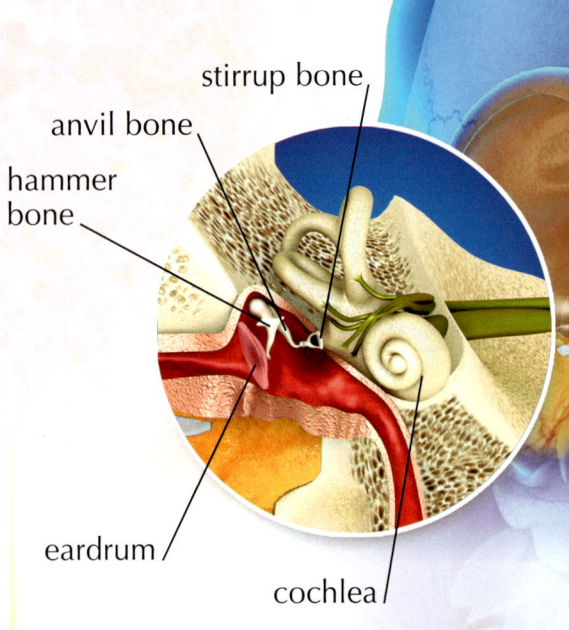

hammer bone
anvil bone
stirrup bone
eardrum
cochlea

cochlea
The part of the inner ear that converts vibrations into nerve signals.

Small muscles move the eye.

Inside the ear
In the middle ear, sound hits the eardrum, causing it to **vibrate**. The vibrations pass to the body's three smallest bones: the hammer, anvil and stirrup. These transfer the vibrations into the cochlea.

Five senses

Your body uses five senses to detect the world around you. Sight and hearing provide your brain with the most information. The sense of touch is found all over the body and it allows you to identify different kinds of pressure, as well as temperature and pain. Taste and smell detect chemical substances.

Structure of the eye
The cornea allows light into the eye. The iris changes the size of the pupil at its centre to control the amount of light it lets in. The cornea helps the lens to focus light rays on to the retina.

The optic nerve carries signals to the brain.

The retina is the light-sensitive membrane at the back of the eye.

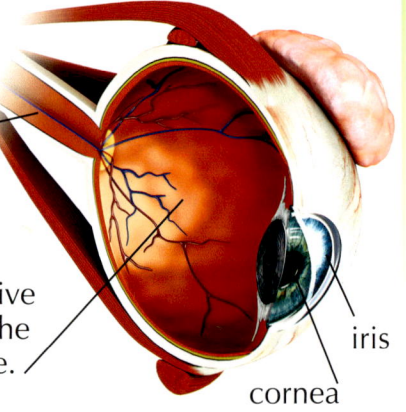

iris
cornea

Reacting to pain

Nerve endings in the skin enable us to sense pressure, different temperatures and pain. If you burn your hand while cooking, signals from the nerves speed through the central nervous system, telling your hand to move away from the source of heat – immediately.

Smell and taste

Sniffing brings air into the nasal cavity. The air, containing scent molecules, passes over the olfactory nerve endings and they send signals to the olfactory bulb. Taste buds in your mouth detect chemicals in food that are dissolved in **saliva**. The taste buds send messages to your brain about the flavours of your food.

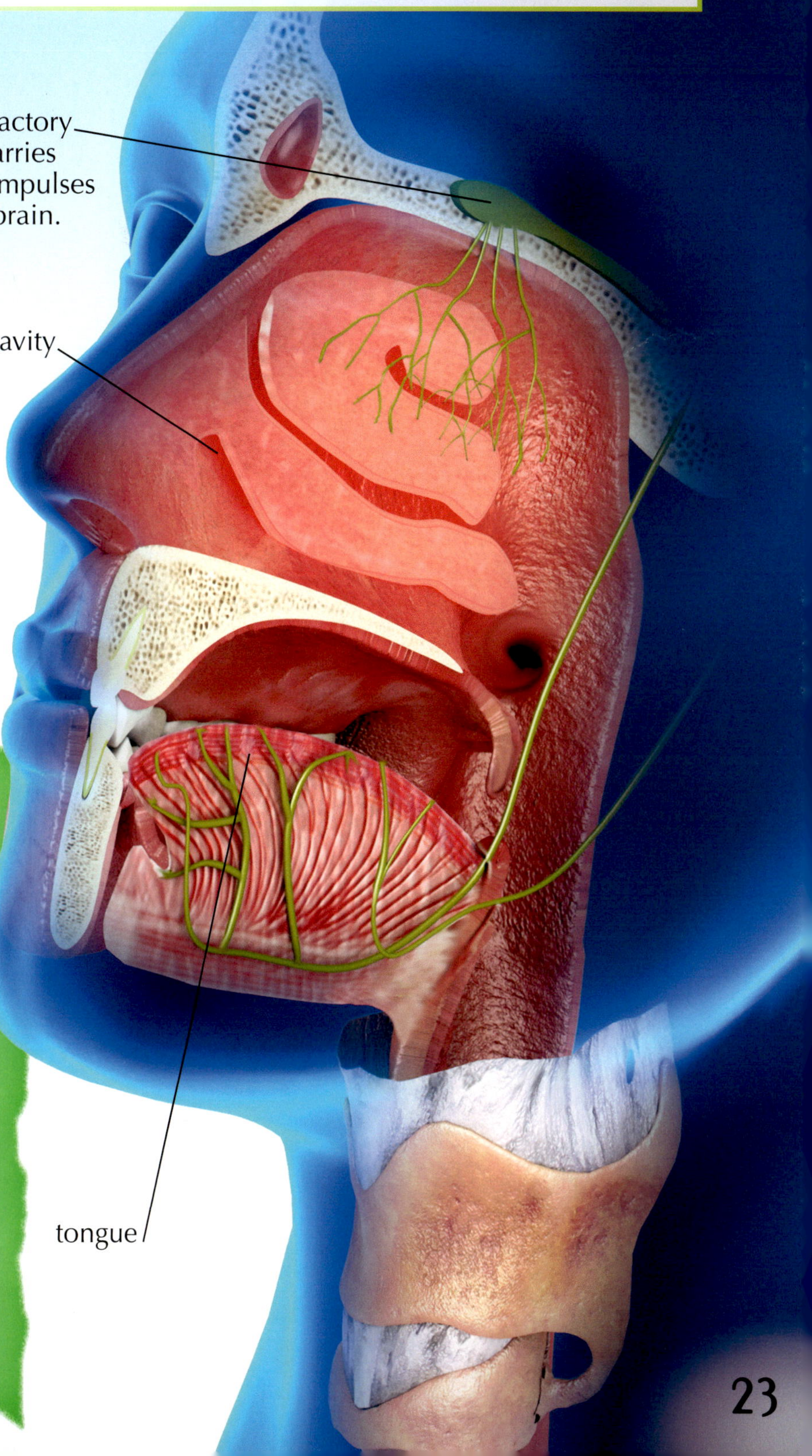

The olfactory bulb carries nerve impulses to the brain.

nasal cavity

tongue

TOP FIVE BITESIZE FACTS

- The iris gives the eye its colour.
- You have about 10,000 taste buds on your tongue, the roof and back of your mouth and in your larynx.
- Smell receptors in the olfactory nerves can distinguish between 10,000 different smells.
- Human eyes can detect up to 10 million different colours.
- Your fingertips and lips are the most sensitive parts of your skin.

What happens to your food?

The digestive system is a long tube running from your mouth to your anus. Its job is to break down the nutrients found in the food and drink you consume so that they can be absorbed into your bloodstream.

The digestive system

Food enters through the mouth and passes into the stomach. From here, it travels through the small intestine, where the nutrients are absorbed. It then passes into the large intestine, before leaving the body through the anus as **faeces**. Attached to this long tube are several other organs, such as the pancreas. These produce special chemicals called enzymes, which help to break down the food.

After swallowing, food enters the oesophagus and passes into the stomach.

TOP FIVE BITESIZE FACTS

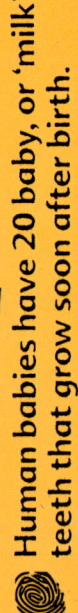

- Human babies have 20 baby, or 'milk', teeth that grow soon after birth.
- As you grow older, your baby teeth will be replaced by 32 adult teeth.
- It takes seven seconds for food to travel from the mouth to the stomach.
- The average adult stomach can hold just under one litre of food and water.
- Every day, your digestive system will produce about half a kilogram of poo.

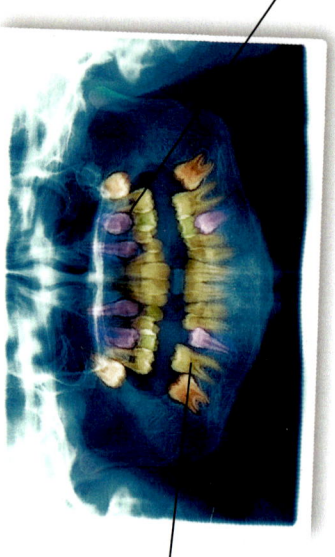

baby tooth

adult tooth

Teeth and saliva

Your teeth cut up and chew food, while your tongue pushes it around and mixes it with a watery substance called saliva. The saliva moistens food so that you can swallow it easily.

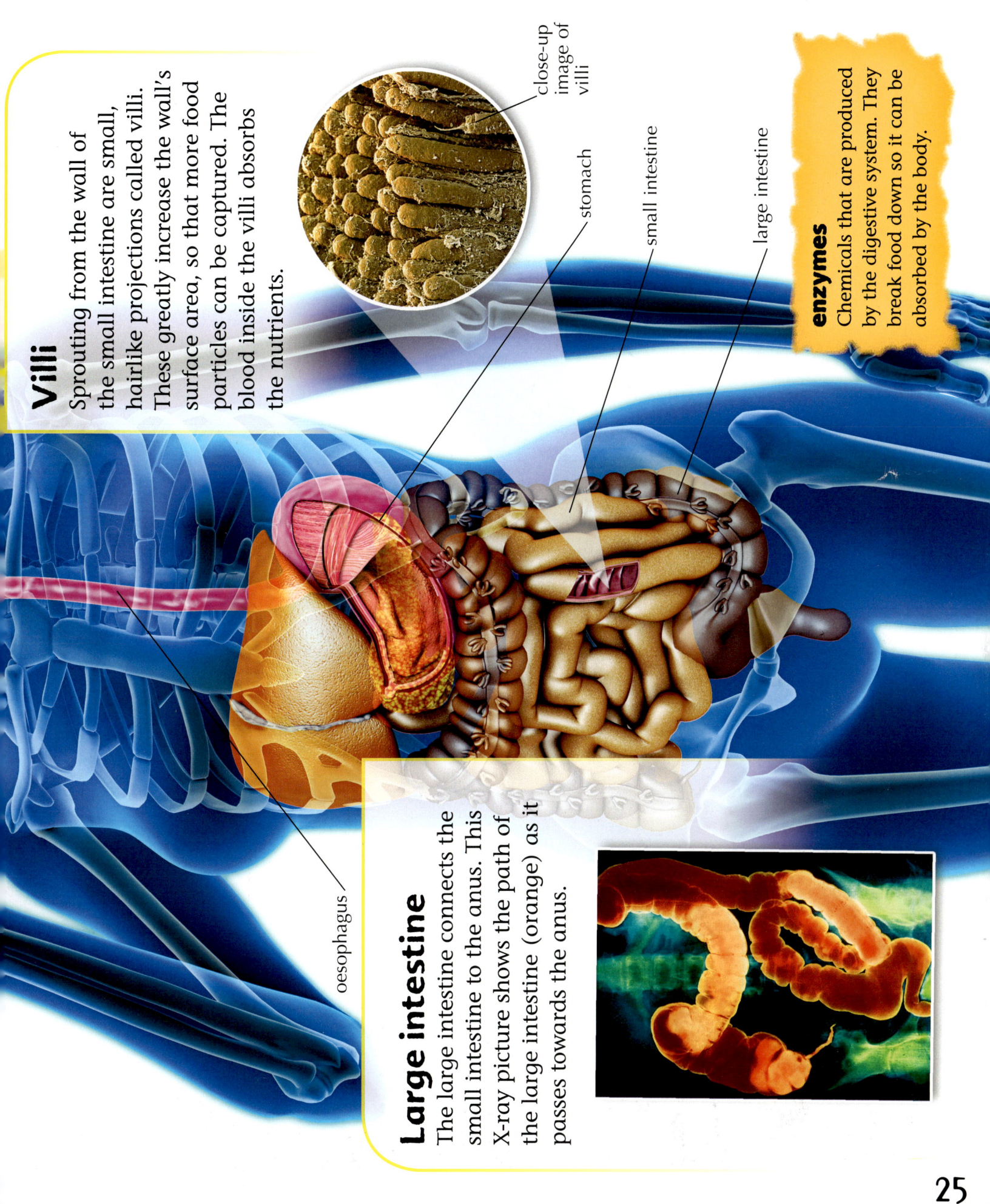

Villi

Sprouting from the wall of the small intestine are small, hairlike projections called villi. These greatly increase the wall's surface area, so that more food particles can be captured. The blood inside the villi absorbs the nutrients.

close-up image of villi

stomach

small intestine

large intestine

enzymes Chemicals that are produced by the digestive system. They break food down so it can be absorbed by the body.

oesophagus

Large intestine

The large intestine connects the small intestine to the anus. This X-ray picture shows the path of the large intestine (orange) as it passes towards the anus.

25

Building blocks

We are all made up of cells, which are often described as 'the building blocks of life'. All human cells are tiny – too small to be seen except through a microscope.

Human cells turn the food we eat into energy. Each type of cell then uses this energy to carry out its own special jobs inside the body.

Inside a cell

At the centre of most cells is a **nucleus**, which controls cell division and reproduction. It is surrounded by jelly-like **cytoplasm** in which **mitochondria** float. The mitochondria give the cell energy, while the cytoplasm transforms that energy for use by the body. A **membrane** surrounds the cell.

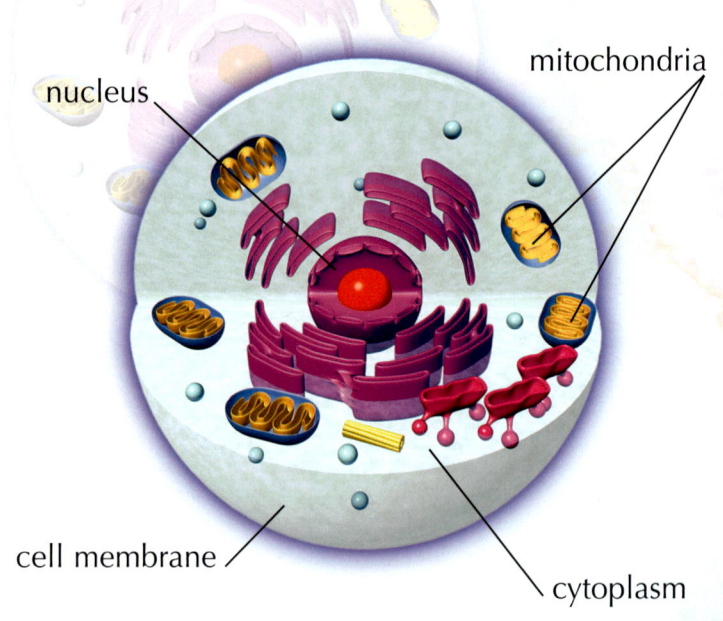

TOP FIVE BITESIZE FACTS

- A human body is made up of about 100 trillion cells.
- The cell membrane protects the cell and controls what can enter and leave the inside of the cell.
- Sex cells are also known as gametes.
- The longest cells in your body are the nerve cells that stretch from your toes, up your leg and into your spine.
- All humans start off as a single cell, which divides inside the mother to become multiple cells.

Cell division

There are two kinds of cell division: mitosis and meiosis. Mitosis happens when the body needs more cells, either for growth or to repair damage. A 'parent' cell produces two exact copies of itself, known as 'daughter' cells, in a process called **replication**. The other kind of cell division is called meiosis and produces sex cells for reproduction.

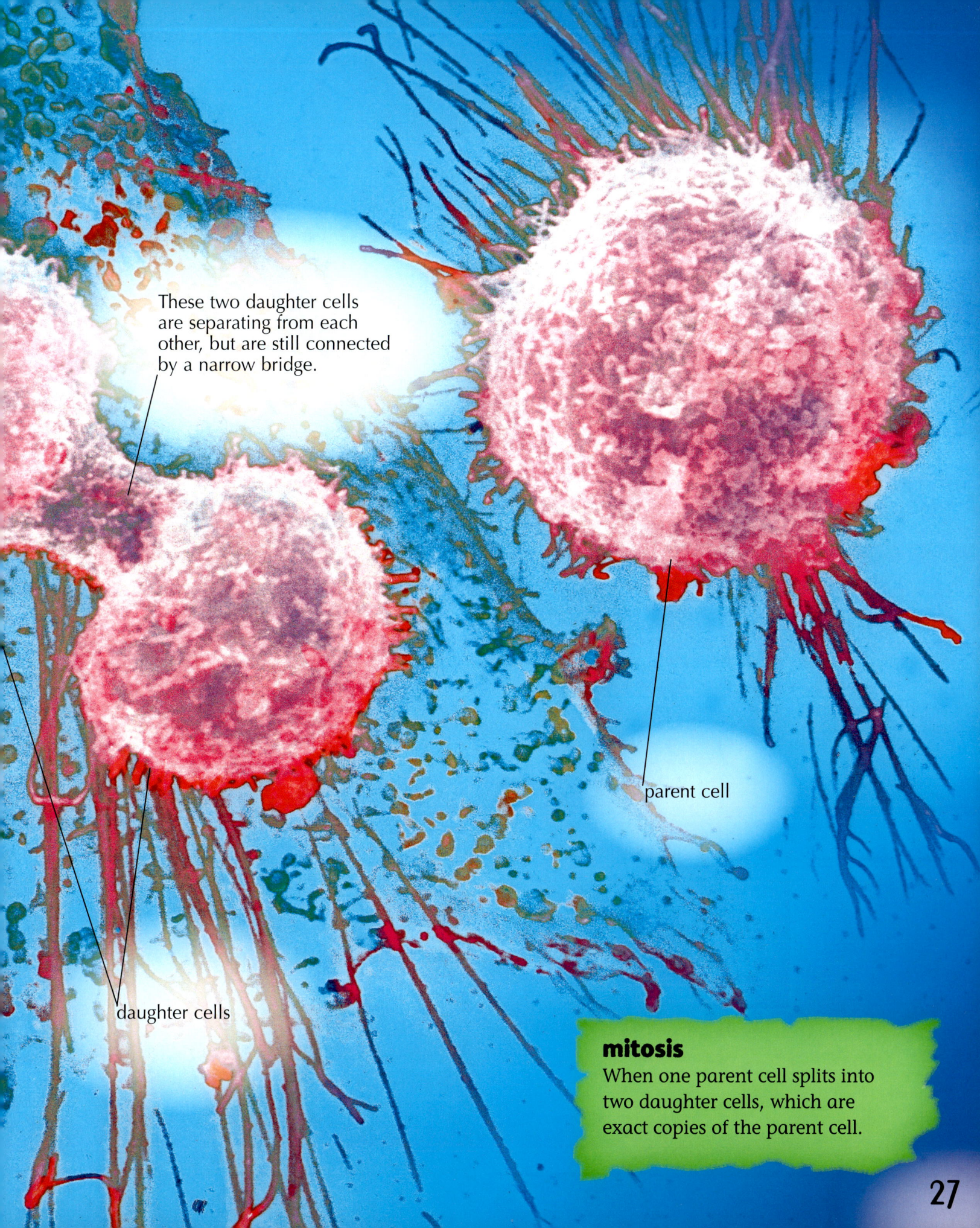

These two daughter cells are separating from each other, but are still connected by a narrow bridge.

parent cell

daughter cells

mitosis
When one parent cell splits into two daughter cells, which are exact copies of the parent cell.

Special instructions

Genes carry the instructions for making your body. Unless you are an identical twin, your genes are unique. You get half your genes from your mother, and half from your father. Genes are stored in the nucleus of all cells, as a special chemical called DNA.

The DNA double helix

DNA is made up of two strands of material intertwined to form a shape known as a double helix. A double helix is very strong because it cannot be broken apart when pulled in one direction. The two strands, made of sugar and phosphate, are linked to each other at intervals across the middle.

Chromosomes

DNA forms long strands called **chromosomes**. The nucleus of each cell contains 46 chromosomes arranged in 23 pairs. One of these pairs are sex chromosomes, called X and Y. These chromosomes decide what sex a person is. Males have one X and one Y chromosome, while females have two X chromosomes.

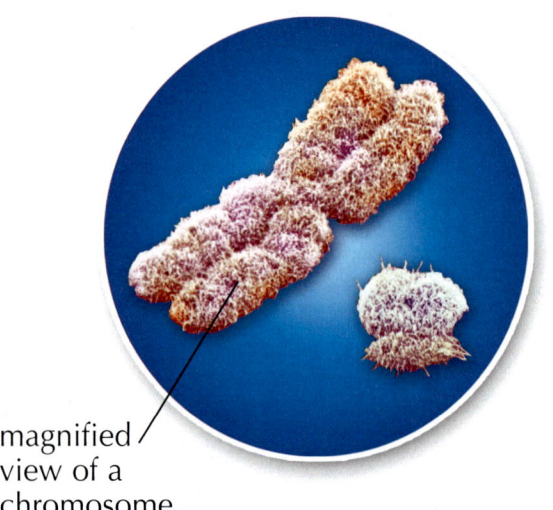

magnified view of a chromosome

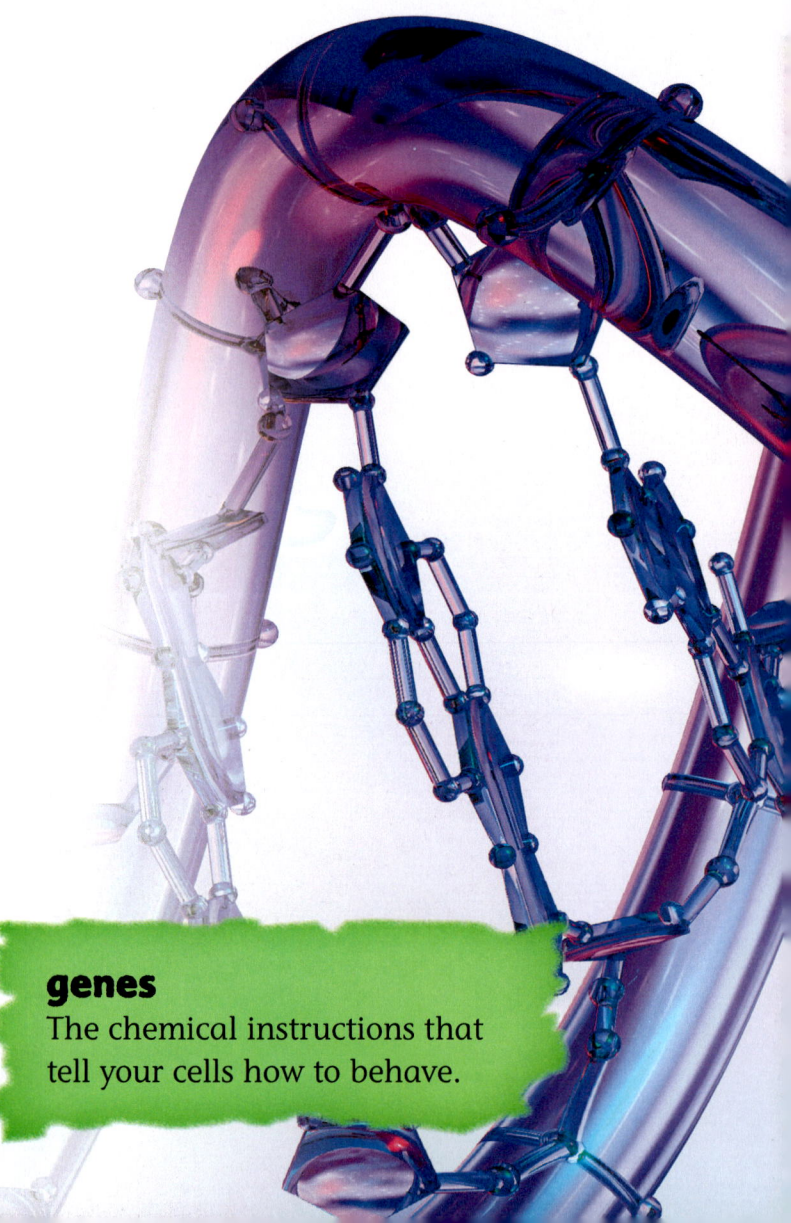

genes
The chemical instructions that tell your cells how to behave.

DNA bases

This computer artwork shows a DNA molecule. When it is pulled out, the DNA double helix looks like a twisted ladder.

TOP FIVE BITESIZE FACTS

- Every human shares 99 per cent of their DNA with every other human.
- Humans have 98 per cent of the same DNA as chimpanzees.
- Humans and cabbages share about 40 to 50 per cent common DNA.
- If you laid out all the DNA from your body's cells it would stretch to the Sun and back more than 600 times.
- The structure of DNA was discovered by James Watson and Francis Crick in 1953.

Glossary

arteries
Thick blood vessels that carry blood away from the heart.

blood vessel
A tube inside the body that blood moves through.

bone marrow
The spongy tissue inside some bones, such as hip and thigh bones.

capillaries
Tiny blood vessels that carry blood to the body's cells.

cartilage
Tough, flexible tissue that covers the surface of bones at the joints and protects against damage.

cell
The basic unit of all living things. A cell is able to reproduce itself exactly.

chromosome
One of 46 threadlike structures in the nucleus of a cell. Chromosomes carry genetic information in the form of genes.

contract
To become smaller or tighter.

cytoplasm
The thick liquid found inside a cell. It holds the cell's parts inside.

diaphragm
The wall of muscle that keeps the organs in the chest and abdomen apart.

DNA
DNA stands for deoxyribonucleic acid – the genetic material of all living things.

faeces
The solid waste of undigested food that leaves the body through the anus.

gland
A group of cells or an organ that produces special substances, including hormones. The body needs these substances to perform certain jobs.

hormone
A chemical messenger that is produced and released by a number of different glands around the body.

keratin
A tough protein that is found in nails, hair and the upper layer of the epidermis.

lungs
A pair of organs, found in humans and many animals, that pull fresh air into the body and release stale air from it.

lymph
A fluid that flows from the tissues to the blood as part of the lymphatic system.

melanin
A dark-brown or black pigment that gives colour to skin, hair and eyes.

membrane
A thin layer of tissue that surrounds the organs.

mitochondria
Tiny structures inside a cell that use food to make energy.

mucus
A thick, slimy fluid given off by some membranes to moisten and lubricate.

neuron
One of the nerve cells that carry electrical signals through the nervous system.

nucleus
The centre of a cell.

nutrient
A substance, such as a carbohydrate, vitamin or protein. The body needs nutrients to grow and work properly.

organ
A part of the body that is responsible for a particular function. The heart, liver and lungs are examples of organs.

perspiration
A salty fluid produced by the sweat glands of the skin.

platelet
A small cell in the blood. Platelets are important for blood clotting.

replication
The process by which DNA makes exact copies of itself when a cell divides.

saliva
A fluid produced by the salivary glands to keep the mouth moist. Saliva begins the process of digestion when mixed with food.

skeleton
All of the bones inside a human or animal's body. The skeleton makes up a creature's shape and protects its organs.

synapse
The gap between one nerve cell and another.

veins
Blood vessels that carry blood back to the heart.

vibrate
To move backwards and forwards extremely quickly.

Index

A, B
alveoli 17
anus 5, 24, 25
arteries 14
atria 14
axon 18, 19
biceps 9
bladder 5
blood 4, 5, 6, 7, 14–15, 16, 17, 24, 25
bone marrow 6, 7
bones 4, 6–7, 10, 11, 13, 21, 22
brain 4, 7, 9, 13, 19, 20–21, 22, 23
breathing 5, 16–17
bronchi 16, 17
bronchioles 17

C
capillaries 14, 17
cardiovascular system 4, 14
cartilage 11, 16
cells 6, 7, 12, 13, 14, 15, 17, 18, 19, 21, 26–27, 28, 29
cerebral cortex 20
cerebrum 20, 21
chromosomes 28
cochlea 22
cornea 22
cranium 7
cuticle 13

D
dendrites 19
dermis 12, 13
diaphragm 16, 17
digestive system 24–25
DNA 12, 28–29

E, F, G
eardrum 22
enzymes 24, 25
epidermis 12, 13
eye 20, 22, 23
femur 7
fibres 8, 9, 10, 19, 20
fibula 6
gametes 26
genes 28–29
glands 12, 13, 16, 18, 24

H, I
hair 4, 12, 13
heart 6, 7, 10, 16–17, 19
hormones 5
infection 4, 12, 15
interneurons 18
intestines 5, 24, 25
iris 22, 23

J, K, L
joints 8, 10–11
keratin 13
kidneys 5
larynx 16, 23
ligaments 10, 11
lungs 5, 16–17
lymph 4

M, N
meiosis 26
melanin 12
membrane 21, 22, 26
meninges 21
microscope 26
mitochondria 26
mitosis 26, 27
motor neurons 18
mucus 16
muscles 4, 6, 8–9, 10, 14, 16, 17, 18, 20, 22
nails 4, 12, 13
nerves 4, 9, 13, 18–19, 20, 21, 22, 23, 26
neurons 18, 19
nucleus 26, 28

O, P, R
oesophagus 24
olfactory bulb 23
oxygen 5, 14, 16, 17
pancreas 24
perspiration 13
plasma 15
platelets 15
replication 26
reproduction 5, 26
retina 22

S
saliva 23, 24
sebum 12, 13
senses 18, 22–23
sensory neurons 18
skeleton 4, 6–7
skin 4, 12–13, 15, 16, 23
skull 7, 11, 21
sperm 5
spinal cord 4, 18, 20, 21
stomach 8, 24
subcutaneous tissue 12
synapse 18, 19

T, U, V
teeth 24
tendon 8
tibia 6
tongue 23, 24
trachea 16
triceps 9
urine 5
veins 14
ventricles 14
vertebrae 11, 21